The Sky Blew Blue

The Sky Blew Blue

by Cora Vail Brooks

A book of exercises in writing and poem
making with examples of solutions

NEW VICTORIA PUBLISHERS, INC.

Box 27, Norwich, Vermont 05055

ISBN 0-934678-13-8

Library of Congress # 87-060700

Library of Congress Cataloging-in-Publication Data

Brooks, Cora.
    The sky blew blue.

    Summary: A book of creative writing exercises intended to stimulate
the production of poems, proverbs, and descriptions, with examples.
    1. English language--Composition and exercises--teaching. 2. Creative
writing--Study and teaching. [1. Creative writing. 2. English language--
Composition and exercises] I. Title.
PE1404.B76   1987   808'.042   87-60700
ISBN 0-934678-13-8

*Published by New Victoria Publishers, a literary
and cultural organization located in Norwich,
Vermont.*

*Typeset by the graphic arts students at Oxbow
Vocational Center, Bradford, Vermont.*

cover photo by Jerry Fish

To two brave teachers
who teach by heart

Barbara Sorenson
Susan Rogers

Acknowledgements

With special thanks to the many students and friends who have inspired and tested these exercises, including children at Speedwell Adoption Agency, New York City; Yale Child Study Center, New Haven, Connecticut; Harvard Epworth, Cambridge, Massachusetts; Dartmouth Hitchcock, Hanover , New Hampshire; Lyme Co-operative Nursery School, Lyme, New Hampshire; students at Hanover High School and Richmond School, Hanover, New Hampshire; students at public schools in Swampscott, Marblehead, Newton, Watertown, Concord and Amherst, Massachusetts; students in Chelsea, Thetford and Norwich, Vermont; students at Wheaton College, Norton, Massachusetts; Goddard College, Plainfield, Vermont; The Institute of Social Ecology, Vermont; Lesley College, Cambridge, Massachusetts and in Chelsea, Vermont around a round kitchen table.

Also I wish to give grateful acknowledgement to Miss Lucus my first grade teacher who taught me to write and to Miss Nerlinger, my fifth grade teacher who was a magnificent and splendid teacher in whose class I promised myself I would become a teacher when I grew up.

"Perhaps there is a moon shining from somewhere, as though behind a hill - just enough light to make out the strange writings, the star charts on the inner walls."

Charles Simic

Table of Contents

Introduction

Poetry is the closest that words can come to nonverbal communication. It is not merely a description of a feeling or a retelling of events , but rather it is an attempt at primary expression using secondary form.

Touching mud, one would have a primary sensation. Reading a description of how it feels to touch mud, one would have a secondary experience of the sensation. The poem of mud would be an expression which would attempt to **recreate** rather than describe the experience.

Because poetry is often highly charged with feeling, it can suggest to children the power of words. Poetry helps a child understand **how** language can work. It is an excellent introduction to language as a tool of expression. It can be used to increase vocabulary, and to introduce reading and writing.

If children become interested in writing and reading, because through them they can be in touch with their own and other people's experiences, they are more apt to be interested in learning the skills of spelling and grammar. To teach the skills of spelling and grammar before children understand their relevance means, in many cases, wasted time for the teacher and the children.

As adults we read the literature of other adults. We find its relevance to our lives. Children reading the literature of other children have a similar experience. Reading and writing can be understood by children as tools which increase an understanding of the world; tools which give us a fuller expression of ourselves; tools which enhance communication. The children read to find something out, to have an adventure; write to express themselves, to explore the possibilities - rather than reading to please a teacher, or writing to fill a page.

A Letter to Teachers

This book is to encourage and inspire writing by giving suggestions of writing exercises which are playful, simple and unusual.

After each description of an exercise, there is an example or there are several examples of a result or results of a completed exercise. If we were a group of people and we were each told to cook an egg, one person might boil the egg, another fry it, someone else might scramble it, and another person might use the egg with other ingredients to make a cake. There are as many ways to "solve" these writing tasks as there are people writing. There are no "right answers." One can play with the writing exercises many times and each time there could be a different result, just as an egg can be cooked many different ways.

The hope for this book is that it will become useful to individuals and groups of people who are interested in stimulating writing in others or in themselves.

Preschool teachers can read the exercises aloud and record the responses children have, to make a poem or a story which the children will recognize as their own. Teachers of children and students who already know how to write can use the book to encourage free expression.

It is a good idea for the teacher using these exercises to do the exercise herself, or himself, in the same time period as the class and with the class.

It would be best *not* to require anyone to turn in or read a solution aloud. These exercises will work best if they are never graded. If students are required to hand in to a teacher or read aloud the results of these exercises it may diminish a freedom of imagination which these exercises are designed to encourage.

Sharing one's writing from these exercises with others should be a **choice** and an **option** on the part of each student.

The first draft of a solution is only a draft and not a final product. Drafts can be made of writing until a student is satisfied with a poem or story. Let students, over a period of time, do several writing projects and let the students choose one or two out of several, to present. Part of good writing is rewriting and editing.

Encourage students or yourself to write the first draft without hesitation or censorship. Then, later, go back to rework a piece, if you wish.

Each exercise in this book can be used for a 40-45 minute classtime period. Ten minutes can be used to set up the exercise, to explain it. Ten minutes can be used to write, and twenty minutes will be left for those **brave** enough to share their results. If the exercises are described as experiments in writing it may encourage students who in the past have been cautious or blocked in their writing, to write.

Oral Poems

These poems are for saying aloud.

Name the females in your family, giving their first names. Start with your own name. Include your ancestresses. Do not identify who these people are, just say their names. Do not worry if you cannot remember everyone.

Sometimes birds sing without taking turns. It is o.k. to let each person who wants to say a name or names to say it or them even if someone else is saying another name or the same name at the same time.

Example: Cora, Oona, Anita, Antoinette, Amelia, Barbara, Marge, Cassie, Katherine, Minerva.

Name the male names in your family giving their first names. Include your ancestors. Begin by saying your own name.

Example: Cora, Luke, Joshua, Tom, Charles, William, Henry, Max, Michael.

If there are several people in your family with the same name, say that name over. It is o. k. to sound like birds repeating themselves.

When everyone is saying names at the same time, if you want to, sneak in the name of someone you love secretly who may not be in your immediate family.

Make up new names for yourself , for your teacher, for your friends.

Example: Little Big Foot, Fast Running Deer, Steep Icy Path, Red Hawk

Do not call anyone a name which might embarrass or hurt them. It is o.k. to be funny or have fun.

Make up new names for the flowers.
Example: little pink ears

Make up new names for the birds
Example: pine tree hopper, yellow bird

Tell the names of your pets, past and present.

Definitions

Make up words from scratch. Do this together as a group or individually. If done as a group, each person who wishes to, could make up a word, or could suggest a letter for a word being made. Make many new words.

Each person who wishes may choose some of the words made up to define. Make up definitions for new words. Choose some of the definitions to read aloud or present. No one is required to do this.

Definitions

retic   is the sound of heat coming
through the radiator
retic,retic,retic

yash   is mashed yam

zilp   is the slippery surface of mud

kyna   is when something is soggy and
lopsided

axsete   is a crude seat made in the woods
from the stump of a tree
and made with an ax

jaquerlo   a round fence made of dried twigs

clymante   a special hat worn by judges to
give them an ordinary person's
look as they leave the court house
so they will not be approached by
the people

vus   a fingernail which has been cut
and is no longer on the finger

pradil   a box some people keep in their
drawer with feathers, stones and
old movie ticket stubs, or the items
themselves

stux   fast finger food

Rock Group

Make up names for a rock group.

Rock Group

The Chelsea Seven
The Dazzlers
The Superlatives
The Founders
The Diplomats
The Outfielders
Ice and Roses
Elbow Oil
Splash Down
Generations
Rib and Whittle
The Unopposed
The Hemlocks
The Fallen Apples
The Whole Length
Antics
Investors
Flesh and Spirit
The New Moons
Ompompanoosuc

Proverbs

Read examples of proverbs. Say old proverbs you know by heart. Make original proverbs, or say old proverbs in new ways.

Avoid clichés.

Proverbs

If we are kind to another
we are kind to ourselves.

We are who we are here with.

If you grow to be a tall person, stand
up to your full height and still do not
look down upon anyone or anything.

For each seed you wish to grow,
plant four.

To admit a mistake is braver than
to go to war.

Those who imagine they can solve
differences with weapons are cowards
and without real resources.

Never loan somebody something
you cannot do without.

Have many ideas but choose a few.

Listen to everyone for the answer
you know in your heart to be true.

The heart with one wing can foretell
things.

What Water Speaks

If possible, go to a river or a stream. Go to the ocean. Listen to the rain. Pour water back and forth. Wash something with water. Drink water. Imagine water in many ways. Then, if you wish, read a poem or several poems to find a poem about water.

What Water Speaks

Sometimes the water cannot wait to
speak, to tell of the days coming and going,
to tell of the long, hard persistent work it
has done to smooth down the rough, sharp
edges of stones.

Sometimes the water wishes it was
as light and as free as a bird flying
above it.

Sometimes the water feels its vast
weight and tries to escape or break
away from itself and crashes then
against a shore.

Half the month the water gossips
about the moon's belly growing larger.
Half the month the water speaks of
an old fox who climbs the mountain
each night and licks away at the
edge of the moon.

Questions

Ask many questions. Ask real questions, play questions, funny and silly questions. Ask simple questions and hard questions. Ask questions maybe no one knows the answers to. Ask wild and fanciful questions.

Questions

How many rays in the rays of the sun?

How many teeth in the mouth of the
moon?

How many stars are reflected in our
hands cupped for water?

How many ghosts in a corner of dust,
a box of rust, a meadow of mist or
a gust of wind?

How many missing wings on those who
can't fly?

And the stars, do they always dance
as they seem to at night, in such
slow elegant steps or do they rehearse
in the day when their light is invisible
to us?

Sky Blew Blue

Make up a poem on a blue piece of paper. Make up different poems on different colors of paper using the color of the piece of paper as an inspiration or influence in the poem.

Sky Blew Blue

blue as a robin's egg shell
blue as the flower blue bell

blue as an afternoon air blue sky
blue as a darning needle fly

blue as the wide blue ocean
blue as a blue water potion

blue as blue sea
blue as a blue green spruce tree

blue as blue flames
blue as blue veins

blue as a bluebird
blue as a blue word

blue as blue wings
blue as blue rainbow rings

blue as blue feathers
blue as blue weather

blue as blue fish
blue as a blue dish

blue as ice, as blue grass, as iris
blue as mountain, blue as stone
blue as blue dew, blue as blue

Tunbridge World's Fair

Once I saw you at the fair.
You're eyes were blue,
or my eyes were blue,
or there in the air above you
the sky blew blue.

The Dream of A Thing

Imagine an ordinary object, one that you could hold in your hands. Imagine that you could take this object to a field where you put it down and leave it.

Imagine that some day you come back to the field and find the object that you placed there.

Know the object has been sleeping.

You are magic. You can tell what the object is dreaming.

In the same way that you can dream impossible or strange things, so can the object.

Write the dream of the object.

A Dream of a Thing[1]

The shoe is dreaming of another shoe
not a different shoe and not the
same shoe.

The shoe is dreaming of its friend
who would make it into a pair.

The shoe dreams of stepping on a
path that is blue like the sky.

It dreams of following the path to
the moon.

It skips to the moon even though
it is only one shoe.

When the shoe gets to where the
moon was it sees that the moon
was nothing but a piece of chalk.

The shoe dreams the chalk becomes dust
and the dust becomes clouds.

A Dream of A Thing[2]

The spoon dreams of swirling
and turning, stirring and
scooping and then being
licked clean.

The tooth dreams of living
in a space as wide as the
space a star lives in.

The bone dreams of terror,
nightmares of dogs and burials.

The eye dreams of his eye.

The Dream of A Thing[3]

The ribbon is dreaming of the moon.
The ribbon is dreaming of tying
a bow around the belly of the moon.
The ribbon dreams it ties itself
tight around the moon and the
moon unties the ribbon with its teeth.
Then the moon grows long wings
of water and floats away from
the ribbon to the far side of the
sky.
The ribbon is left flapping in
the sky and doesn't know why
and doesn't know why.

Dream

Write out a dream you have had. Write it from beginning to end or from end to beginning. Write the middle first or write whatever detail or segment you can remember.

Dream

In one dream my legs were a lever. They moved as if they were a gate which lifted itself up to open and came down to shut.

They were like half a gate at a railroad crossing.

They were a gate to a dark room.

In another dream somebody had agreed to store my car. When I went to find the car, the tires and body were missing. The things inside the car were missing too. More than the car, I missed my shawl.

The Four Tongues of the Wind

Think of the wind.
Think of the wind as having four tongues.
Say what each tongue speaks.
Choose what one tongue of the wind speaks
and read it aloud with three other people who
have written this exercise and each chosen what
one tongue of the wind speaks to read aloud.

The Four Tongues of the Wind

One tongue speaks of the fish in
a dish and the eyes of stars and
the stars' eyelashes.

One tongue speaks of the green
grass, green leaves, green ice and
the great green steps up the
mountain.

One tongue says hello and hello
and hello,

And one tongue says it is tired
of speaking and refuses to speak.

This is Not

With chalk on a board, a stick in the sand or a
pencil on paper, make a large abstract drawing.
Each person who wishes to continue a line begun
by another person may do so. Each time the
drawing begins to suggest a recognizable form, try
to divert the drawing from becoming
representational.

Do not suggest the purpose of the drawing.

When each person has had a turn to add to the
drawing, the drawing may be considered to be
completed. Look at the drawing for awhile.

Write what the drawing is not. Write as
quickly as you can to try to have your words
come from your pencil or pen before you censor
them. Spill your words. Write run-on sentences if
you wish. Freely associate.

Do not prohibit your imagination. Select some
of the things you write to read aloud if you wish.

Your work is your own. You need not share it
or show it, if you choose not to.

If we free ourselves to explore in writing,
sometimes we may go places and find things we
did not expect to find. Sometimes this exploration
results in finding ourselves writing words we
didn't mean to write, but wrote to find, further on,
the words that finally meant what we wanted to
say.

Sometimes we do not mean anything with our
words. It is o.k. to play with words and have fun.

This is Not²

this is not the kidney of a whale
mixed up with an intestine which
looks like spaghetti which is almost
wrapped around the bomb the whale
didn't swallow because there is no
whale and no bomb

neither is there lightning striking
the bomb and setting it off so
that the whale is blown apart
from its insides and neither is
there a huge lipped water animal
with a mouth like a puzzle piece
and a forehead like a mountain
coming after the innards of the
whale

this is not a map confused or a
confusing map or a balancing
act by a person who wears
her hair as wavy as a W, nor
is this a balloon or a spoon or
a door or a floor

This is Not[3]

It is not a rooster's comb, a building's
dome, nor the foaming of the sea. It is not a
fire or a wire, or a tired woman making an
inquiry, not a nap or a lap, a slap of a river
or a shivering child, not something bold or
wild, not a last will, a feather or a quill or a
chart of the weather; nor is it a map of a
bird's flight, moon or moonlight, eye or
eyelash, pie or piece of pie. Neither is it
well and water, not someone shouting for
order or gasping for breath. It is not a heart
broken in three, the lunch of a mouse on
the porch of a house; not a dance without a
dancer, nor a riddle without an answer.

This is Not[4]

It is not a green full tree in a
shell pale dawn, not an ocean
fit to the horizon, not an apple
or a dappled hill, a loon calling
or the bells at noon, or the water
of a river washing down stones.

Neither is it the light reeled in
from the first evening star
on which I make a wish
to be where you are.

Two True Things

Write a true thing simply and expand. Write another true thing and expand.

Two True Things

I have a house.
The house is old.
It shakes like an old person.

Sometimes my house
seems so old, it feels
like it is no longer living.
It seems like it is a ghost.

I have two children.
Sometimes I miss them
the way I miss summer
in winter, or the way
I miss daylight at night.

I Am

Gather together many objects - a marble, a bell, a candle, a map, a bone, a toothbrush, a glove, a long piece of string, a hammer, an eraser, a pencil and other things. Have each person choose one thing. Each person who wishes may choose a thing while blindfolded.

Then write as if you are the thing speaking.

I Am[1]

I am the map with rivers
and roads, snakes and toads,
trucks with loads.

There are mountains with
paths and streams.
There are clouds and ponds
without any seams.

I dream I am a tablecloth
spread out over the land.

I dream I am a road decorated
for a peace celebrating band.

Without going to war
we decide not to have war anymore.

We sing and dance and play on the street.
We wear ribbons in our hair
and ribbons on our feet.

I Am[2]

I am a little red box with many
little paper stars.

Four stars are silver, one star is
gold, three stars are blue, one
star is green.

The silver stars dream of dishes
and spoons.

The gold star dreams it is very far away.

The three blue stars dream they are
water in a pond and the green star
dreams it is grass.

I Am[3]

I am the glove dreaming of
being a dish or a fish, a
tool or a fool. All day in my
dream, I wave. I wave at the
birds, at the people, at the
dogs, at the sky. I wave
at rabbits and eggs and worms
squiggling by.

I wave at leaves of trees and they
wave back to me. I wave at the
flowers, the toad and the bee.
I wave in the street, I wave
in the yard, I wave at my
neighbor, I wave at the guard.

I wave right side up and upside
down, I wave in the country
and in the middle of town. I
wave at the stars and I wave
at the moon. I wave in February
and I wave in June. With mittens
and scarves picked up from the
ground, when I'm done waving
I'll join an old lost and found.

I Am[4]

I am the hat dreaming of the fog that
comes to sit on my head like it is a hat.

I Feel Like

*Pick an object that you can say you feel like.
Expand. If you said you felt like a stone, qualify
how it is that you feel like a stone. Are you a stone
in a wall, or are you a pebble being skipped over
water?*

I Feel Like

I feel like one of the bricks
in a brick wall on a school
building. I feel fixed in place,
surrounded by other bricks.

The sun shines on me and I
cannot sweat. I do not grow.
I do not move. I am one of
the ones who holds up the
wall. My removal would
not make the wall tumble,
but if I was not there, someone
might say the wall is breaking
a little, or in need of repair.
Would I rather feel like the red
clay, unformed, by the river -
unscooped, unmolded, unfixed?
Sometimes I think so.

This Flower

Pick a flower or imagine a flower. Say what each petal stands for.

This Flower

This flower, picked between the
afternoon rain and the evening rain
is yellow and bellowed, billowed and
pillowed with petals.

Each petal is a woman or a man
growing from the center. Each
petal is a song or a tune or a flap,
a limb, an arm, a leg or maybe
an organ or muscle, a liver, spleen,
lung or heart.

The whole crowd of petals
settled here on this flower.
They open like a window or
like summer.

On This Piece of Paper

Give everyone a piece of paper. Say the words that get written on the piece of paper are magic.

"On this piece of paper there are words that are magic. These words can......"

On This Piece of Paper

On this piece of paper there are words that
are magic.

These words can hide from the fire
the whole time the fire is burning.
These words can burn and still be
spoken. These words are glass and
can break, these words are knives
and may wound, they are flowers
that may bloom, birds that may fly.

These words can be mixed up with
other words and say something clear.
These words can be transparent and
say things which are obscure.

These words can fight and sting.
These words can turn, bend, list,
fall, mend, follow, signal and forgive.

Forgive these words, they are not birds.

Group Poem

One person in a group begins a poem by writing one line on a piece of paper. Then that person passes the paper on to the next person. The second person writes a line which continues, expands, contradicts or freely associates with the first line. The second person then folds back the piece of paper so that only one line of the poem (the line the second person wrote) is showing. The second person then passes the paper on to the third person who writes the third line of the poem and before passing the paper on to the fourth person, folds back the second person's line so that only one line, the third line, is showing. The fourth person continues this process.

Anonymous Group Poem

The flowers were darkened with blood and tears

The black wood
was wet with rain and
night was coming
along the road to castleton

I met a bear

hoddy hoddy ho ho
hee hee hew hew

chuckling together they ran
through the lab

it was raining as they went
and they put up their umbrella

it was big
and covered the pig's wig

Size

Writing on different sizes and shapes of paper can sometimes stimulate originality.

Short Poem

A bird sings a song
Song isn't long
Sings it
Never gets it wrong.

Paper Bag

Write on the outside of small paper bags. Write what is inside the bag. (The bag is magic and can contain anything, stars or elephants.) Write instructions on the other side of the bag about how to use what is in the bag or how to open or not open the bag.

Bag Poem

Inside this bag
there are words
which can mend
things stronger
than where they
were torn.

Open the bag
after talking
with a good friend.

Group Word Poem

Ask everyone to contribute a word if he or she wants to. Ask everyone to write a list of the words contributed. Each person makes a poem or a story out of the words given and any other words which may be necessary to the story or poem.

Example of Group Word Poem

words given: blue, snow, whirl, breath, wonder, longing, sanctuary, bequeath, searching, leap, riding, edge, clarion, seam, soothe, rest

Playing

Now these words are searching for rest
they whirled down to us
and fell like a breath
or like the blue snow

We wonder at our longing
for them, thought them to
be caught in some sanctuary
where we were not allowed

They bequeath to us our searching -
our leaps over the edge
and our riding on the edge

We make a seam between them
with other words - a song in a clarion
voice and they spill and still fill us,
soothe and move and show us what
we have known all along but knew not
how to say.

Chant or Spell

Make up a chant or a poem to find something which is missing or to make something happen which you wish to happen or to protect you from harm. A spell.

For Protection

In order to protect yourself against a
mishap on Friday, the 13th, you can

hold up three fingers
to the sky and turn
around three times
each time folding in
another finger -

then you can hop
on one bare foot
singing a song
you can't remember
the words of, making
up new words as you
go along

then you can dig a hole in the ground
and break three eggs into the hole
and add fifteen pieces of bark
and two pieces of a puzzle that
already has pieces missing

then dust the house
and add the dust

then stir with your nose
until you sneeze

Dizzy

Turn around ten times.
Write how it feels to be dizzy.

And the Sky Turned

And the sky turned,
the house slid aside,
the ground was moving,
do you remember?
We were turning ourselves
around to find out
what we could say
about being dizzy.
It was the last day of summer.

We had talked about
the moon, how it hides
and slides aside, it was
a disc, a shallow bowl of light.

We had talked of the earth
and how she turned, wobbled
and revolved.

We had thought of the last
thing we thought of the night
before when the moon was full,

and I thought of making
you a poem as perfect
as the moon.

About the author

Cora Brooks was born April 9, 1941 in New York City. She has children named Oona and Luke. Once she had a cat named Blacky. She had a dog named Ydnas Elwot, a dog named Fierce and a cat named Bum. She lived in a big city, a suburb, a small town, a small city, a medium sized city and now she lives in Chelsea, Vermont. She has taught at many different schools. If she had nine more lives after this one she would like to be a gardener, a painter, a piano player, a singer, a dancer, a lesbian, a journalist, a photographer and a private eye. If she were an animal she would be a grey squirrel. When she grows up she wants to be like her son or her daughter.

photo: Debra Walter

Other Books by Cora Brooks

Heather in a Jar *Pomegranate Press, Cambridge, MA. 1973*

Ransom for the Moon *Acorn Press, Chelsea, VT 1978*

A Cow is a Woman *Acorn Press, Chelsea, VT, 1979*

The Moon is a Skull of Dust with Dark
Wings *Acorn Press, Chelsea, VT, 1980*

Poems for a Book of Hours *Acorn Press, Chelsea, VT, 1980*

Posey and the Professor *Acorn Press, Chelsea, VT, 1981*